I'm really fed up with this cleaning job! I'd love to audition for the Follies, but I'm sure we wouldn't get parts.

I bet we would! I'll bet you *all* the money in my piggy bank that we can get parts in the Follies.

Auditions
Today

Fairy Tale Follies

For the Philpot family   G. P.

Text and illustrations copyright © 1994 by Graham Philpot

All rights reserved under International and Pan-American Copyright Conventions. Published in the United States by Random House, Inc., New York,
and simultaneously in Canada by Random House of Canada Limited, Toronto. Originally published in Great Britain by David Bennett Books Ltd. in 1994

Library of Congress Cataloging-in-Publication Data

Philpot, Graham.

The fabulous fairy tale follies / by Graham Philpot.

p. cm.

SUMMARY: The reader is given clues to find those chosen in auditions for characters in eleven fairy tales, including "The Three Little Pigs," "Snow White,"
"Jack and the Beanstalk," and "Puss in Boots".

ISBN 0-679-85316-2

[1. Characters and characteristics in literature — Fiction. 2. Acting — Auditions — Fiction. 3. Picture Puzzles.] I. Title.

PZ7.P55Fab 1994

[Fic] — dc20   93-30479

Manufactured in Singapore 10 9 8 7 6 5 4 3 2 1

FABULOUS FAIRYTALE FOLLIES

GRAHAM PHILPOT

RANDOM HOUSE 🏠 NEW YORK

Okay, everyone. The first audition is for the Three Little Pigs. We'll start in five minutes. Can someone call the Little Pigs and the Big Bad Wolves? And hurry up with that brick house and the trees for the dark forest! Come on down, George. I need your help with the boards.

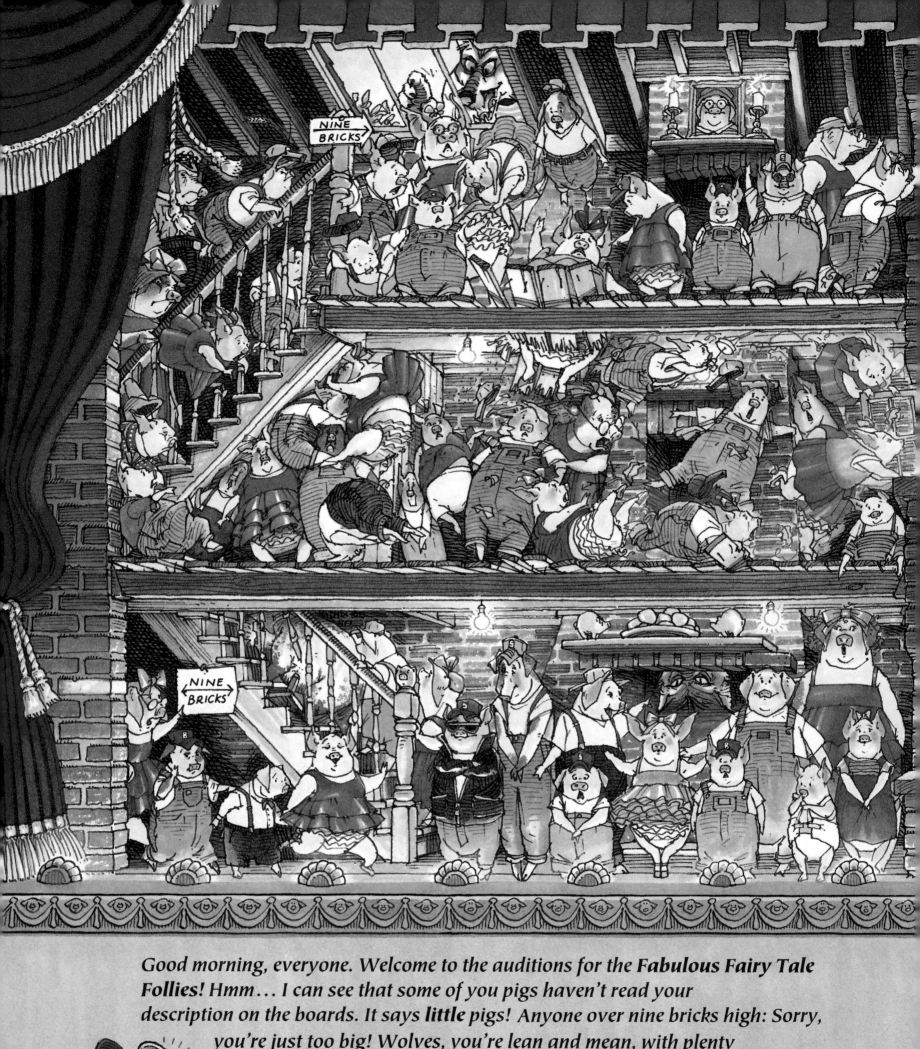

Good morning, everyone. Welcome to the auditions for the **Fabulous Fairy Tale Follies!** Hmm... I can see that some of you pigs haven't read your description on the boards. It says **little** pigs! Anyone over nine bricks high: Sorry, you're just too big! Wolves, you're lean and mean, with plenty of huff and puff. No, no – I said blow the house **down**, not blow it up! George, is that your pig up there, with brown ears and a yellow dust cloth?

NINE BRICKS

NINE BRICKS

Twig-House Pig
- Pink bow on head
- Short frilly red dress
- Frilly white petticoat
- Pink shoes

Big Bad Wolf
- Black-and-white porkpie hat
- Blue-and-white striped sweater
- Red suspenders
- Blue jeans
- Black-and-white basketball shoes
- Yellow eyes

THE **THREE LITTLE PIGS**
Straw-House Pig
- Blue baseball cap
- Yellow T-shirt
- Red suspenders
- Blue jeans

Brick-House Pig
- Red-and-white baseball cap
- White T-shirt
- Blue overalls with rec label

Okay, Little Red Riding Hoods. Let's see you skip happily across the stage.
You're off to visit Granny, who's not herself today. Wolves, I know you're
supposed to be hungry, but remember – *you're only acting!*
Hey, George, is that you in the tree?
And did I just see your pig go by?

MAXIMUM HEIGHT

MAXIMUM
HEIGHT

GRANNY'S
HOUSE

LITTLE RED RIDING HOOD
Little Red Riding Hood
- Red cloak with hood
- Green dress with white apron
- Red shoes
- Basket of blue and yellow flowers
- Curly red hair

Wolf
- Small round glasses
- Pink spotted nightgown
- Pink spotted nightcap
- Purple shawl
- Orange eyes

Girls: You're in the Three Bears' cottage, and you're acting as though you own the place.
Bears: She's eaten your porridge, she's broken a chair, and she's slept in your beds – you're not at all happy. Altogether now:

"Who's been eating my porridge?"
I see you've been in the costume box, George – and your pig, too!
Will you both **please** get off the stage?

GOLDILOCKS AND THE THREE BEARS

Goldilocks
- Long golden hair with pink bow
- Blue dress
- White blouse
- White petticoat
- Pink ballet toe-shoes and white socks
- Small brown bowl of porridge

Mama Bear
- Medium brown fur
- Yellow shawl and apron
- Blue dress
- Round glasses

Baby Bear
- Light brown fur
- Red-and-yellow striped vest
- Black pants

Papa Bear
- Dark brown fur
- Black hat
- White shirt
- Blue-and-yellow striped vest
- Red bow tie

Now, all you Cinderellas – it's midnight, you're supposed to be home, and you've lost that famous glass slipper. Ugly Sisters, I want you to be ugly with a capital UGH!

George, I can see you – that outfit really doesn't "suit" you. Now, where's that pig of yours…

CINDERELLA

Cinderella
- Blond hair
- Pink feather in hair
- Blue-and-white ball gown
- Pink handkerchief
- Small glass slipper
- Long white gloves

First Ugly Sister
- Short and fat
- Orange hair with yellow bow
- Round glasses
- Pink-and-green ball gown
- Purple gloves and yellow fan

Second Ugly Sister
- Tall and thin
- Purple hair with yellow feather
- Half-moon glasses
- Purple-and-green ball gown
- Pink gloves

Listen, Snow Whites: You've been abandoned in the heart of the forest,
and you have a strange feeling that you are not alone.
George! Get up off your knees and "Hi-Ho" off —
and take that pig with you!

SNOW WHITE AND THE SEVEN DWARFS

Snow White
- White bonnet
- Shoulder-length black hair
- Brown apron and shawl
- Blue dress
- Small brown boots

Chief Miner
- Bald
- White beard
- Round glasses
- Candle
- Big hammer

Major Miner
- Bald
- Gray beard
- Oblong glasses
- Miner's lamp
- Pickax

Minor Miner
- Looks like George
- Brown coat
- Bowler hat
- Pipe
- Miner's lamp

Leprechaun
- Green top hat
- Green tailcoat
- Yellow feather
- Long nose
- Tin whistle

Pirate Pixie
- Yellow-and-black hat
- Red-and-white spotted bandanna
- Black tailcoat
- Wooden leg

Pirate Mate
- Floppy red pointed hat
- Long red beard
- Blue-and-white socks

Pixie Pixie
- Tall red hat with white spots
- Slanted eyes
- Gray goatee

Come on, you Hansels and Gretels. You're meant to look really hungry and miserable! Witches, you are horrible, greedy hags, on the lookout for something tasty for the pot.

George, stop hanging around – just get off the stage!

And don't forget that wretched pig!

HANSEL AND GRETEL

Hansel
- Blue-and-white peaked hat with tassel
- Short brown hair
- Blue jacket with white collar
- White pants with blue checked patch
- Brown boots

Gretel
- Yellow floral bandanna
- Yellow floral apron
- Green shawl
- Brown dress with blue checked patch
- Small clogs
- Empty basket

Witch
- Tall black witch's hat
- Purple gloves
- Half-moon glasses
- Blue shawl
- Purple-and-orange tights
- Black buckled boots

Cat
- Black fur
- Red eyes
- Green collar

Okay, cats. Puss in Boots is a real rascal: He's clever, he's cunning,
he's the coolest cat in town. Ogres, you're ferocious but foolish —
the king of the castle!

     Oh, no — "Pig in Boots"! What's next?
     George, if I have to tell you one more time...

PUSS IN BOOTS

Puss in Boots
- Black fur
- White tip on tail
- Black-and-red hat with big yellow feather
- Yellow-and-green vest
- Blue mittens
- Black-and-brown boots
- Sack tied to stick

Ogres
- Golden Viking helmet with horns and jewels
- Fur-lined brown vest
- Fur collar
- Blue belt
- Red-and-yellow striped pants
- Reddish brown beard

Aladdins, you're a poor peasant boy who discovers an ancient magical lamp in a secret cave. Genies, you are the slave of the lamp, ready to grant Aladdin's every wish.

I wish that George and his pig would disappear!

ALADDIN

Aladdin
· Chinese hat
· Pink shirt
· Purple tunic
· Baggy blue pants
· White ankle socks
· Black-and-white pointed shoes
· Old brass magic lamp

Genie
· Curly black eyebrows and beard
· Red vest with gold trim
· Gold earring in left ear
· Yellow feather
· Baggy yellow pants
· Curved golden sword
· Purple sash

Ladies and "gentlemen"! Beauty has fallen in love with the Beast, and together they are about to joyfully dance the night away. Mind your toes, ladies! Beasts, you just can't wait for that good-night kiss!

George, you really are turning into a bit of a "boar"! Apologize to that young lady, find your pig, and get off the stage!

BEAUTY AND THE BEAST

Beauty
- Black hair
- Tall yellow cone-shaped hat
- Long pink-and-green dress
  Purple cape attached to wrists
- Red pointed shoes
- Red rose in hand

Beast
- Yellow sleeveless jacket
  with black fur collar
- Yellow rose on collar
- Green-and-purple tunic
- Red shirt with blue bow tie
- Red belt

Come on, Billy Goats Gruff – lots of trip-trapping across that
rickety old bridge, please. Trolls, you're really fed up.
All that tripping and trapping is driving you CRAZY!
George, you're driving *me* crazy!
Now take that pig and trip-trap
off stage – IMMEDIATELY!

THE THREE BILLY GOATS GRUFF

Big Billy Goat Gruff
· Big curly horns
· Blue baseball cap
· Cream-colored fur jacket with brown collar and cuffs
· Collar with bell
· Long gray goatee
· Oblong glasses
· Dark blue pants

Medium Billy Goat Gruff
· Slightly curly horns
· Cream-colored fur coat with black spots
· Gray skirt
· Pink hat and handbag
· Round glasses

Little Billy Goat Gruff
· Tiny horns
· Blue-and-white striped T-shirt
· White shorts
· Red baseball cap

Troll
· Blue hat with barnacles on it
· Seashell horns
· Pointed ears
· Seaweed hair
· Green skin with pink spots

Okay, this is the last audition. Boys, you're Jack, a spunky young fellow
with a bean for a brain, but BOY can you climb that beanstalk!
Giants, let's hear you roar:

> "Fe, fi, fo, fum, I smell the blood of an Englishman!"
> George, I'll have that pig **and you** for dinner if you don't both
> **GET OFF STAGE RIGHT NOW!**

JACK AND THE BEANSTALK
Jack
- Yellow hood
- Brown bag with shoulder strap
- Gray-green tunic with belt and money bag
- Yellow sleeves
- Baggy red tights
- Sandals with crisscross strapping

Giant
- Red hood
- Gray-blue tunic with horn toggle buttons
- Belt with silver buckle
- Black beard
- Three teeth
- Golden chicken on shoulder
- Golden harp

Congratulations! You have all been chosen to be the stars of the
Fabulous Fairy Tale Follies.
Give yourselves a big round of applause!

Well, we tried, my little friend!
Maybe next time.

It's not fair!
I should be up there!

By the way, how much money *have* you got in your piggy bank?

You wouldn't *really*
take my money, would you?